WE'VE BEEN PUT THROUGH FIRE

& Come Out Divine

Stories of Hope & Survival

Mary Simmerling, Ph.D., Editor

Contributions by the Writers of *Write Where We Belong*

 AMHERST WRITERS & ARTISTS PRESS

Published by: Amherst Writers & Artists Press, Inc.
P.O. Box 1076
Amherst, MA 01004
Phone: 413 253 3307
www.amherstwriters.org

ISBN 978-1-987813-83-8 pbk
ISBN 978-1-987813-84-5 ebook

DEDICATION

This book is dedicated to the staff and volunteers at RAINN (Rape, Abuse & Incest National Network). As survivors of sexual violence, we want to honor and express our deep gratitude to RAINN's many volunteers and staff, who have worked and continue to work tirelessly on behalf of survivors of sexual violence, their families, and communities. Without their dedication and hard work the organization would not be what it is today. We also want to thank and honor RAINN's founder Scott Berkowitz, without whom the organization would not exist.

Since its founding 1994, RAINN has provided services to more than 4.3 million people. RAINN's victim services programs serve an average of more than 300,000 survivors and their loved ones each year. RAINN created and operates the National Sexual Assault Hotline, available by phone at 800.656.HOPE (4673) or online at online.rainn.org in both English and Spanish (rainn.org/es). The online chat also has a quick exit feature that provides immediate protections during its use. RAINN's hotline services are free, confidential, and available 24/7. RAINN's victims' services, public policy, education and awareness, and client services programs prevent sexual violence, help survivors, and ensure that perpetrators are brought to justice.

To learn more about RAINN, visit RAINN.org.

CONTENT WARNING

This book contains explicit descriptions and discussions of sexual abuse, domestic violence, and rape, some of which involve minors. The material can be distressing and triggering for some readers, particularly those who have experienced similar traumas or know others who have. It is important to note that this entire book deals with the topic of sexual assault, and pieces that are triggering to one person, may not be triggering to another. Please proceed with caution and consider your personal comfort and mental health. If you feel you may be negatively affected by these themes, it may be best to avoid reading this book or to seek support while doing so.

Remember, it's okay to put the book down if it becomes too much. Your well-being is important. If you need help, please reach out to a trusted individual or professional. There are many resources available for those affected by sexual violence, including RAINN's National Sexual Assault Hotline, which is available by phone at 800.656.HOPE (4673) or online at online.rainn.org in both English and Spanish (rainn.org/es). The chat also has a quick exit feature that provides immediate protections during its use. RAINN's hotline services are free, confidential, anonymous and available 24/7. You are not alone.

Reader discretion is advised.

TABLE OF CONTENTS

FOREWORD

I first got to know Mary Simmerling a little over a year ago. And as soon as I met her, I also began to hear about the workshops she was facilitating with the group "Write Where We Belong" and RAINN. Not, of course, anything specific—the work done in these workshops is always confidential. But she would sometimes come to committee meetings still glowing from hearing the pieces that had been written in her recent workshop. It was immediately clear to me that she cared passionately about this work and, as I read the book you hold in your hands, I completely understand why.

The individual poems and stories in this book document rape, other forms of violence, trauma, toxic behavior (mostly male), misuse of power, and some of the worst aspects of the patriarchy. They explore the loss of identity, agency and voice when one is a survivor of that kind of violence. Many of the early pieces in this book have a terrible weight and gravitational force. The reader can feel the damage done through misuse of power and force, and the way the particular incident of rape and violence hold victims in trauma's enduring shadow for years to come. We know that sometimes survivors are paralyzed by the event indefinitely.

But not these writers. What you hold in your hands is an unflinching testimony of the damage done by abusers, but also a testament to the strength, vitality, courage and resilience of survivors. The arc of this anthology moves from documenting the terror and violence of the traumatic event toward reclamation of self through owning and directing the story.

It is often said that we cannot choose the events of our lives or what happens to us; all we have control over is how we respond to what happens. These writers have chosen to respond with agency and creativity. In the final pages of this book, these women articulate their own manifestos—how they will live going forward. To rephrase the end of Keena's poem, and the title for this book, "They have been put through fire, and have truly come out divine."

When I heard that the group was considering publishing an anthology, I immediately hoped that Amherst Writers & Artists

1

Press could be involved in getting these words out in the world. This is exactly the kind of project we want to promote. Pat Schneider, our founder, had a long history of social justice work through writing. Part of the reason she founded AWA was to make sure that the stories that don't normally make it to publication with literary presses would be represented. As I write this, I can feel her at my shoulder applauding.

As current chair of AWA, I couldn't be more delighted than I am to help to midwife this anthology into a world that needs these words of rebellion, reclamation and resistance.

- Sue Reynolds,
Chair, Amherst Writers & Artists
Port Perry, Canada

"in realization
we don't exist without each other
she says: there's nothing about you
i'm not willing to know"

Leanne Betasamosake Simpson,
"Head Of The Lake"
Theory of Ice

INTRODUCTION

As a writer and survivor of sexual assault, I know firsthand the healing powers of the creative self, accessed through writing alone and in groups, and through sharing one's writing with others. And I've long known that I wanted to lead writing workshops with other survivors. There is a significant body of literature and research that demonstrates that individuals are indeed able to change through the creative power of the self. Recent research suggests that sharing stories about one's own traumatic life experiences can be healing for survivors of violence and trauma, and that art and writing can play an important role in that healing. For example, utilizing expressive writing as a positive psychology intervention for trauma survivors has been shown to be meaningful in their healing. James Pennebaker's research has demonstrated that expressive writing can allow trauma survivors to find meaning through writing. And, of course, language is itself a powerful tool that conveys emotion, carries moral import, and can create a sense of belonging or community feeling. As van der Kolk notes in *The Body Keeps the Score,* "Language gives us the power to change ourselves and others by communicating our experiences, helping us to define what we know, and finding a common sense of meaning."

Having worked with RAINN as a volunteer for many years, I knew that it was exactly the right organization to partner with for these workshops. RAINN offered to send an email to members of its Speakers Bureau inviting them to contact me if they were interested in joining my writing workshops where no prior writing experience was required. The women whose writing you will read in this book came forward to join me on this creative healing journey.

As the leader and facilitator of the group, it was important to me to establish and maintain a safe space for writing and sharing that writing. Early on, I was asked by one of the writers, *What if I don't remember every detail exactly — should I still write that?* I reminded the group that we were there to engage in writing as a craft. We were not there to write testimony or testimonials. We were not even there to write specifically about the assaults we suffered. We were there to engage in expressive writing in response to prompts.

To weave together words from our memories and experiences. To utilize metaphor and poetry to narrate and shape our stories. What we wrote would not be assessed or judged for accuracy. These were our stories. We get to write our own stories. We get to use our own voices, to speak our truths, and use our personal experiences and memories to find and reclaim our own voices.

And thus I came to realize three things essential and remarkable about writing with survivors of sexual assault and domestic violence:

- Our voices have been silenced for so long.
- We have been told that our truths aren't true, and that even if they are, no one cares anyway.
- And in response, we have hidden, made ourselves small, and become silent and invisible.

As the weeks went on, I marveled as I listened to the writing created in the workshops. I was astounded by the quality of the feedback that was provided. And I was humbled when, after asking the group if they wanted to continue meeting, they looked at me and asked how long I was willing to continue hosting the workshops. And so we agreed to keep writing together as a group until we no longer had anything left to write. Although we had initially come together as survivors, we stayed together as writers. As one of our founding members would later say about the workshops, *I love coming to the workshops because through them I am able to discover what it is that I have to say.* And so it was that we came together every other Monday afternoon to discover what it was we had to say, and to share our stories.

Now in our second year, "Write Where We Belong" has evolved into a group of profoundly talented writers who exemplify the power of story and care deeply about writing as a craft. Through these workshops, we have discovered the ways in which writing and sharing our stories empowers us as individuals and members of communities. We have experienced the many ways our stories can bring us together and create a sense of belonging, allow us to discover what it is that we have to say, and to bear witness to each other. Our stories help to shape and inform how we think about each other and the world. They stimulate our innate creativity and open us up to new ways of thinking about things that might never have been considered otherwise. Indeed, our stories have the power to change history– both the future through prevention and the past through reclamation. Through our individual and shared stories we are able to forge bonds, make space for each other, and create ourselves anew. Through these workshops, we have discovered the hopefulness and sense of belonging that can come from writing in community with others. As Pat Schneider, who developed the AWA method, observed in *Writing Alone and with Others:*

> "When we write, we create, and when we offer our creation to one another, we close the wound of loneliness and may participate in healing the broken world. Our words, our truth, our imagining, our dreaming, may be the best gifts we have to give."

Through writing together we have also come to realize that we are not defined by what has happened to us, but rather that we — and we alone — have the power to make our own meaning of our experiences. This idea — that we alone are in control of deciding how we will incorporate and give meaning to our life experiences and share our stories — has the potential to shift the locus of control not only of our individual but also our communal stories in powerfully disruptive ways. We have the power to take back and own our own stories. And in so doing, we can bring to light some of the many harms associated with victim-blaming mythologies that further disempower survivors of sexual assault by falsely suggesting that the victims themselves rather than perpetrators are responsible for their traumatic experiences.

We hope that as you read our stories, you will gain deeper insights into the far-reaching and long-lasting impacts of sexual violence, as well as the healing processes for survivors. And for those who read our words and see yourselves reflected back, know this: We see you. We hear you. We believe you.

– Mary Simmerling, Ph.D., Editor
Ottawa, Canada

Live

I have been a fighter my entire life
My gloves are sewn into my hands
An accessory I must match every day
The need to justify everything — every way.
Each battle adding character I didn't need
They needed a flower when I was only a seed.

Alcoholics and fighters teaching me to be tough
If they weren't bleeding, you didn't go hard enough
Snitches get stitches — there's a line in the sand
Lessons would hurt, but grow up, be a man.

Sixteen on my own selling for fast cash
All to go to a school that tried to deny my ass
Move to high school number 3 after my MIP.

Hello, Florida gulf coast — now it's parties I see
Working all the time — too busy to graduate
No one was even around for the date.

Knocked down but never kept down
Through adversity I am inspired to rise
Making it through was never a surprise.

See — I have been a fighter all of my life
My gloves are sewn into my hands
And now that I am no longer boxing
I know it might be had to understand
These gloves have kept me alive —

But maybe I need to do more than survive.

4 Walls

4 walls, no door
In the corner, on the floor
Angles point away from me
Zero degrees and empty

Flat white, beige or eggshell
On fragile cracks we walk to hell
No one hears me say
I hurt so very deeply today

No mommy, no daddy
We all kids in this family
Creepies creeping, hot fires swell
Sink down deep under the well

Overflow of hate soils,
Hot paint sears, stings and boils
Alone in my scorching corner I hide
Four walls crispy, ashes dried

A fire burns
Our hell turns
Brushes cooled, varnish me small
Plastered flat on the wall.

The mystery of a single shoe

Ever wonder, the history behind a single shoe lying in the street? Surely there must be a story attached to it—or even a tragedy. For humans, two shoes allow for balance, an unspoken confidence, a sense of equality even. Losing a shoe can be a very personal dilemma—especially when you feel as though you're navigating life shoeless.

On a winter night in 1984, my perpetrators stood inside a college dorm and watched as I crawled on the floor desperate to find that one lost shoe. Five hours past my curfew, my disheveled appearance would be telling enough to my then-young parents, yet the reality of my bare feet would tell a tale of shame that would take 35 years to recount.

Silenced

Feeling trapped by sleep, my eyelids heavy from the weight of alcohol, I struggled to stay awake as bright fluorescent lights shone down on my exposed bare body. Boys or men I had never met before surrounded me, with an audience of football players watching. As I dressed, my eyes spoke what my mouth could not. I could hear nothing but my mind screaming as the pain of shame and humiliation consumed me. My sense of self shattered. My voice stolen.

What I was wearing

Was this:

From the top
a white t-shirt
cotton
short-sleeved
and round at the neck

This was tucked into
a jean skirt
(also cotton)
ending just above the knees
and belted at the top

Underneath all this
was a white cotton bra
and white underpants
(though probably not a set)

On my feet
white tennis shoes
the kind one plays tennis in

And then finally
silver earrings, and lip gloss.

This is what I was wearing
that day
that night
that fourth of July
in 1987.

You may be wondering
why this matters

or even how I remember
every item
in such detail

You see
I have been asked this question
many times
it has been called to my mind
many times
this question
this answer
these details.

But my answer
much awaited
much anticipated
seems flat somehow
given the rest of the details
of that night
during which
at some point
I was raped.

And I wonder
what answer
what details
would give comfort
could give comfort
to you
my questioners

seeking comfort where
there is
alas
no comfort
to be found.

If only it were so simple
if only we could
end rape
by simply changing clothes.

I remember also
what he was wearing
that night
even though
it's true
that no one
has ever asked.

Breath

The weight of my child's future squarely on my chest
Each inhale a struggle lacking more than just breath
But there is no time he is angry — feelings have to wait
My heart sprinting out of my chest — my ribcage a gate.

Goosebumps and pins and needles down my spine
"I'll call 911 if you kick this door one more time!"
Can't think about dying with a newborn in your hand
But his kicks are getting stronger — Mama's gotta make a plan.

Where can I hide you while he beats me — what a real man
Maybe I can distract him long enough to calm down
His temper is only lost with me, never around town.

Threat of police makes him kick rocks, not the door
Telling his family and friends stories devoid of his gore
Still they have to answer for the company they keep
The pseudo-shepherd tending his sheep.

How many women's lives will it take
For you to realize you made a mistake?

Flight

Is he coming back?

I am rushing, I feel anxious
Agitation rising, heart racing

Am I forgetting anything?
Have I looked everywhere?

A litany on repeat in my head
Frantically making mental checkmarks

I open the closet one more time
Reaching up to search the top shelf with my hands

...

My diary... My pictures...
My first poems...

He didn't steal everything from me.

Ignis Luna

By the fire gettin' warm
Rememberin' how the hell was born
Hands of hate, charred hearts don't care
Hell's Predator arrives in ice cold air

Our moon up high, then and now
Same world turns reminds me how
Soft clay molded, pulled from fire
Layered strength surrounds me higher

Higher, higher our full moon goes
Glowing sphere elevates my woes
Harden where I ought and
soft where I'm not

Despite his plan
Out the inferno, I ran
Lunar protection, my need of light
A hand up provided that dark night

Blaze loses power
With each passing hour
I won't stay crispy or cold from pain
I am not ashes, I overcame.

Power

What he did was so bad
Little ears can't hear

They come with questions
Whose answers I fear.

Ones that might break them
Or take the spark from their eye
My little innocent eternal happiness
I can't be the one to make you cry.

Maybe I'll say he was mean to Mommy
And he was mean to you
His parents were mean to him —
But these words just don't do.

The baby was Mom's immortal power
And I named him as such
That man is nothing to you
You are the light he could not touch.

Glitter

Who invited the Giant Queen with all her magic spells?
High on vapors o' gin and clouds of smoke to hurl her bitter pills.
She poofed herself here, far away from her tomb.
Maternalized in the flesh of our delivery room.

Why bring a girl into the world?
Her father despised; that coward, unfurled.
Spat, "He didn't want you, little fetus of dueling hates."
Now two weeks overdue, a girl's unwelcoming awaits.
Hold your breath, our Queen desires all the air in the room
But who's loudly unheard from her liquid womb?
The queen proclaims, "He cried like the unborn.
O' sad day your birth we all do mourn."

Early morning, a scent so hostile, a prick, a sting, up her
        pointed nostril.
"I declare war on this rival," A Queen's seething at the
        delivery's arrival.
Who dares push out my joy of winter?
Down the halls, her splitting screams splinter
As out pops the fresh brown bud of late February,
Little girl wrapped tightly, prepared to bury.

"This one is rejected! Damn this girl to hell!"
Spinning wicked words, she casts her spell.
The queen's staff, raised
All allies caged
"Go! Summon all my demons to agree.
Prepare to die if you differ from mummy!"

To hell, to hell, spinning we fell,
To hell we go, to hell we went,

tumbling together, swirling the drain,
Two drops twisting, oil and rain.
Dozens of Dollar Store glitters she buys —
they shimmer, they shine,
her magic invented for hate so divine

Powers that wane as my body grows;
A mother's hate exponentially unfolds.
My voice, my cry — like dad's — too deep,
Notice, awareness begins to creep.
My eyes that turned from green to brown,
My cry almost kept her from nights on the town.
The food we need, paid in alcohol.
The clothes outgrown, too fat after all.
The bottles I dump, you refill again.
My morning, haunted by pain of disdain
A hangover gifts you sweet amnesia.
Drunken words from last night's diva.

Your harem of gory men I cursed and sent away.
A girl protected by God, left in harm's way.
My mouth sasses back, when I start to see through.
I grow, and I see. Whew.
Just a tiny, wicked, queen, and it's you.

Disappear

Sky spits
Hail hits
Brain splits
Run away pain
I want to become the fog

Flowing molecules
Able to linger
Allowed to un-fuel
Absence of anger

Happily out of gas
Or anyone on my ass
Dew on grass
I settle on the road and sit

I want to become the air
Translucent
Intangible
Avoidable
Indivisible
Invisible
Invisible-er
– Alone–

Pop, pop, hail hits
Sting of my return
Skin and bones too heavy
Want too much

A girl too many
Pain too heavy
Muscles grow weary
Brain gets busy

Melt into fog

To whom to tell
To go away empty
simmer there,
alone like air

Desperate to disappear.

A good place to rest

As I woke up, I forgot where I was. As I looked around, I took it all in. A solid metal door with a slit of plexiglass for a window. There was a steel bunk above me, three concrete walls with no color surrounded me. A sink and a toilet that were connected to each other. Next to my bed was a steel desk that was attached to the wall, and a tiny steel stool attached to the desk. As I put my bare feet onto the cold concrete floor, everything came back to me — the horrors of what brought me to this place of solitary confinement. I didn't know what day it was, couldn't even tell what month it was. It had seemed as though I had slept for days, maybe even weeks. As I stood in this dark concrete box, I slowly walked to the tiny mirror that was above the sink on the concrete wall. I took in my reflection of a person I didn't recognize: long, matted hair, a hideous orange jumper that covered my bony frame. As I touched my face, the reality sank in — that this was real, that this, unfortunately, wasn't a nightmare. As I laid back down on my blue, thin mat, with no pillow, I wanted so bad to close my eyes and return to the peaceful sleep that I had just woken from.

Forgive and forget

Forgive and forget
Is cyclical thinking
All give and no get
Such a cycle worth breaking.

Stopping the circle
Does not mean to forgive
And the privilege to forget —
Too many nights I relive.

Searching for a reason why
A way to make you the good guy
I believe you were a victim, too
But we are what we repeatedly do.

There's comfort in what I know to be true
Even at my worst — I could never be you.

Crime scene

This is what we do:
we mark it off
with yellow tape
DANGER
POLICE
CRIME SCENE
GET BACK
STAY AWAY
CRIME SCENE
DANGER
KEEP OUT.

And then
when it's over
we tear it down.

Since
(after all)
no one lives there
anymore.

Who would
live there
who could
live there
after what happened.

Tear it down.

No one
lives
there
anymore.

This is what I did:
I put my clothes
back on
my body
after he was done with me
and then
I left.

(that is
I have been trying
to leave
but I am stuck here
won't anyone help me
tear it down.)

GET BACK
STAY AWAY
CRIME SCENE
DANGER
KEEP OUT.

Little pink purses

She has a bunch of those little pink purses. Each of them free of any contents, unless you count sweets. Some are sticky from candy the men give her. On Sunday afternoons we get dropped off by a new boyfriend, stray neighbor, or creepy uncle who shouldn't have keys to our car, but he does. The ruinous chauffeur pulls up to the movie theater parking lot, on the opposite end. He slows down and before stopping, he says something over his shoulder to his little girl passengers.

"Get out. Somebody will be back here to get you later."

We have been dropped off here lots of Sundays, so we know "later" means two hours, four hours, or six hours. Whenever they want, whenever they are done with Sunday drinking. Someone should remember "the girls." Somebody drunk will be tasked with the chore to pick us up from the dollar day at the movies.

While at the movies, Little Pink Purse Princess and I would wait in the dollar matinee line and try not to talk to the many strange strangers. The men who came alone and sat at the back of the theater or tried to sit by us when they realized we were alone. When it was our turn to pay, I stretched to stand on my tiptoes. I would give the girl our two dollars and say the name of our movie all wrong. The lady would laugh at me and give me our tickets.

She had a cute routine of digging in her pink purse, pretending to look for cash. She was four years old, and I was nine. The men who gave me the bad feeling turned left when we turned left, and turned right when we turned right. We were seeing the same movie in the same theater.

So we take our seats. Princess and I run for the front row. That is the best place. No poofy hairdos or tall men to block our view in the front row. And the creepy men don't want to sit there usually. We play with the up down part of the seats, making them go up and down and up and down. We look back at all the creepies going to the back of the theater because it's fun and because if you act bratty, no bad men want to sit by you. They think you will tell. When they look at us they smile and lick their lips, we turn

around and sit low. They stare at the tops of our straight brown
hair, all messy from the bath we didn't take. The movie is good.
I keep my eyes wide and turn my head sometimes to make sure
they don't make a move to come down to our part of the theater.
Today they don't, but you gotta make sure they see you watching
them.

When the movie ends, we run out fast to the hallway. With
only two dollars, we can't pay for another dollar movie. So when
ours ends, we know that somebody has to check for the car. I tell
her to follow me. We go to the end of the hall with the people
leaving to peek out the windows. I tell her to wait here and hold
the door. I go out to the parking lot and look all around while
keeping an eye on Little Pink Purse Princess- Oh no, I don't see
her purse. No car here either, not yet. I head back into the theater
and some grown-ups have a mean look for me.

"Where is your purse?" I ask.

"Oh no!" she screams.

I realize this is a good reason to go back and we will look for
her purse. It won't look suspicious or like stealing another movie,
but we are. We head back into the theater and go straight to the
front row. No purse. She starts to cry. Not because it's gone but
because she feels shame and because I am mad at her for losing
it again. Now I feel ashamed, for being mad. I don't say anything,
I just take her little hand and we go back into the hall to sneak in
another movie. We repeat this every two hours, checking out front
for a ride home, or sneaking into another movie.

We saw a lot of movies, some we probably shouldn't have, and
my sister left a lot of empty pink purses in those theaters.

The signal

This is what we'd do:

first, we'd collapse our upper body
ever so slightly
with just a tilt of the back
a wilt of the neck
and a drop of the chin

and we'd push our lips out
lower lip leading, just so
as if we were blowing a kiss

and we'd lower our brows
and squint our eyes
so that we'd almost look dark

and then finally
we'd pull our lips in again
quickly
almost imperceptibly
except for the slight lift
at one corner of the mouth

punctuated by
a moment when
for just a second
our eyes would lock together

and then
almost immediately
it would be gone
having taken only a matter of seconds
from start to finish.

This is what we'd do
when we were little girls.

This is what we'd do
to warn each other
that he'd been drinking

standing there beside him
unable to speak for ourselves
unable to change our world

we'd use the signal
if only just to let the other one know
that what was happening was real.

Drifting

This wave breaks against my heart
Crashes through my eyes
Roars in my ears
Threatening to wash me away

I'm drifting
Sand no longer beneath my feet

How do I navigate when there are no stars?
How do I find home when the beacon no longer shines?

The glimmers

I glimpse joy
just as it shimmers away

The glimmers
slipping through my fingers

I stretch to hang on and feel nothing.

While I was sleeping

I didn't know him
I saw the lights come down the driveway
I didn't recognize the car
I was asleep.

There were three dogs that jumped out
They had big brown leather collars
With spikes
And holsters
For their knives.

My dog wasn't there
But I wasn't afraid of the man
Or his dogs and their knives
I was asleep.

And then I remembered about that book
The one where the men come and kill all of the dogs
All of her dogs
In the dark of the night
While she was asleep
Just before they raped her.

I didn't have a dog back then
And even if I had
It wouldn't have been with me there on that night in LA
I was asleep
But woke to the weight of him on top of me
Holding me down
Forcing himself inside me.

I wondered about the dogs' knives
I wanted to ask them

What are they for?
Why are they attached to your collars like that?
But I was asleep.

We were asleep the night he came for us
My son curled up alongside me
The dog in her bed downstairs
No one made a sound that night.

It was the birds that finally woke me
And the morning light over the river
The images from the dream still vivid in my mind
I looked out the window to check for tracks in the snow.

The other day I remembered floating up into the sky
Somewhere in the Catskill mountains
I had been holding onto something that carried me up into the air
Weightlessly, effortlessly, I floated
I can't remember now whether it was even real
Or just an artifact of all of those times I'd had to leave my body.

Art just isn't worth that much

My grief gathers at completion,
each celebration an elegy
the matriculated moment comes at an incalculable cost, an infinite
   regression of anticipation.
What had I hoped for before hope had hardened against expecta-
   tion?
Before beginning, anticipate the unceremonious end.

Her

I would never forgive myself
For not trying to bring her back
They say it's wasted effort, it's foolish
But it's merely perspective they lack.

They'll say it's impossible —
She's already dead
I'll try to revive her until the day that I die
If that's true just take my life instead.

Say it's no use — it's pointless to try
But I can't be just another person walking by
She has come back from hell, she will do it again
Always finding the light — making it her friend.

She can sit in her darkness and quell all her rage
Then explode it a lion released from her cage
She's done it before and she'll do it again
There is no darkness she cannot ascend.

Memories of who I was before will never sway
I know that I'll get back to her someday.

Malibu

He was wearing board shorts
(It was a pool party, after all).

A blinding smile
(With preternaturally white teeth).

A faint dusting of white powder
(Just beneath his perfectly sculpted nose).

Bare chest puffed out with pride
(Strong arms resting on his hips just so).

Bare feet
(Because, of course, he was at home).

I remember his curly brown hair
And his energy.

His strong jaw
The way Malibu backlit his frame at the pool.

And, of course, his sister's room, down in the lower level
With the fan blowing ever so slightly overhead.

The weight of his body tearing me from sleep
My own confusion about what was happening.

(Why was he doing this?)
(Why wouldn't he stop?)

And the fan —
The way it just kept going.

 And then nothing
(In the dark, all wolves are hunters).

Agnosia

Declarative memory deleted, procedural memory impaired.

Act as if. Assemble the story. Act as if.

I had written you the morning before.

I wrote you again not long after.

I write you now as night becomes morning.

I write to keep you close. I write to make a window for us to gaze
through. I write to remember. To reassemble. I write to resist
dissembling. I write to recover. I write to invite response. I
write for relief. I write to make a map in the space in between
us, to make light in the dark with words and want. I write so
my body can imagine safety, safety enough for sleep.

Declarative memory, semantic memory, procedural memory,
aphasia, agnosia.

I return again in the night the fading dark and the drawing light.

Your gift

Your gift — not a gift to me

Play pretend and pretty dresses
Toy ponies and pampered tresses

Coddled, loved, all pretend
To his will we all must bend

Pretend, pretend, pretend

Your gift — not a gift to me

Your gift — a curse that sacrificed me.

Everything

"If I could go back and do it over again, I would change nothing."

That's the expected mindset. No regrets. Everything happens for a
    reason. God has a plan. Hardship is our greatest teacher, and
    all the other trite platitudes we've been taught to ingest and
    then regurgitate, ad nauseam.

I protest. I rebel. I throw off those chains of victimhood hidden
    within toxic positivity.

I would change everything I possibly could so as not to experience
    a life of daily trauma.
I will not attempt to package neatly the senseless acts of violence
    perpetrated against me to make my pain palatable to the
    masses.

I won't assign meaning or value to harm.
I will look right at it,
acknowledge it in its fullness,
in its incomprehensibleness.
I won't put bows on it.
I won't pretend I am better for it.

Every single time we assign value to harm,
we reassert that it must have happened for a reason.
And if there is a reason, then we can't possibly take steps
to keep it from happening again.

I would change everything if I could.

Grammar lessons

She wanted it
was asking for it

(did you see
what she was wearing)

had it coming
to her

(did you see
how she was walking
out alone
after dark)

deserved
what
she got.

Raped.

Choose rape.
The grammar just won't allow it.

Even if
we do.

Even if
we cannot
stop
thinking this way.

The language
rejects

this distortion.

Cannot accommodate
this conception
of rape.

She
wanted it
was asking for it

(did you see
the purple bruises
in the shape of his hands
all along
her lovely neck)

had it coming
to her

(did you see
the way she walked
afterwards
hunched over
a posthumous attempt
to protect her insides)

deserved
what
she got

(did you see
her eyes
like vacant pools
I wonder did she drown
in all those tears).

Haiku.1

Don't call it incest.
It is sexual assault.
Violence and rape.

American dream

She said
(incredulously)
you're so pretty
you don't even need
to go
to school
(what a waste).

He said
(longingly)
you're so smart
(makes me want
to fuck you)
I'd love to
read your work.

The Jezebels

I told my story today to a Christian man with kind blue eyes. He said he's a follower of Jesus all his days. My story is my testimony, but not an easy one to tell. Our conversation turned to girls who leave his church and go to hell. Girls who are not his problem. The short shorts-wearing girls, discovering who they ought to be. Girls from bad homes, without parents, leaving his pews empty. The girls pop into this place for what reason I do not know. Discovering who they aren't when the ladies call them ho's.

I warned him, "Sir, they leave this church when they feel judged and cast aside. Called, "Jezebel", behind their booty-shorted backs, by Pharisees who lie. Women clothed in gossip and feigning modesty. Christian posing ladies prostituting honesty. They spread rumors from their faces, swines swirling in skirts longer than the knee. "Godly women" spinning whispers on the backs of those in need. You call them what you are, isn't that how it goes? Those girls hear, but so ashamed, anger helps them go."

I warned the sinless man as he hid under his facade, busily pimping papers, pretending to do his job. "Preacher man, you are losing girls for God in all this mess. Mister, they will turn red-hot judgment around and call you 'hypocrite.' Christian leaders turning their backs to light up hate for what they fear. Torching judgment from the pulpit landing squarely between those girls' ears. Windbag of Bible verses blowing youth away. Dousing green faiths to wilt a poison onto girls' blooming days. Those young ladies feel tossed and cast aside by your hypocrisy. You lead, not to Christ, but to the hot fear you feel today. What about their children, will they raise them in salvation's residue?"

Slyly, he confided a deviant idea to me, "It is perfectly natural to turn away when a girl comes to my church and looks a certain way."

A nudge. A smirk. From the corner of his mouth he verbalized sideways. "You know, it's awkward to talk to her. So naturally, she goes away."

He was confused, I thought. He thinks we both agree. "I don't know, Sir." I reminded him what my Bible likes to say. "Those girls and their families need Jesus, too. Don't make them walk away! Girls who come here just as they are, short shorts and all, are looking for a welcome, not a judgment call. If they come, let them grow, not fall. Is hope for faith with you here, too? Grant them years to build a relationship they pursue. Maybe they will not wear what makes you feel provoked and ashamed, or maybe they will, and then who are we to blame?"

In pursuit of truth, I opened my Bible. A verse appeared for us to settle and give a solid pathway: Matthew 18:9. "And if your eye causes you to stumble, gouge it out and throw it away.". "Also, Sir, I saw you sneak a pic of her with your cracked little screen today."

The time was right, and I was ready. I told my story today to a Christian man who looked confused. He thought we were the same, but now forgets my name. "We are different, sir. My family rode a crooked path. A road wound wonky, my life cut in half, never easy. I entered a church like this, and the pastor was queasy. Raised by wolves, a girl unwanted. Did I wear short shorts when I was seeking Jesus? Undaunted, I could not recall. Grateful I found Him despite it all. A lost little girl who hurt like hell. I went to the church and found the same spell. Women in long skirts whispering and twitching at the mouth. Arms crossed, brows low, the pastor distracted, just a frivolous mouse. I looked up and saw… nothing. So I left, too, and found my own way. God loves me still; and more today, no, He never turned me away. I was them, and they are me, and your gracelessness hurts God, you see?"

The man with kind blue eyes pressed his pants as he shifted, discomforted in his wooden chair from the words I had gifted. The camaraderie quickly stopped. He gazed right through and he coughed. He stood high above me in my chair. I felt so small, to the floor I stared. The meeting he called was over now. "Thanks for stopping by. You'll have to go," he muttered a lone, powerless reply. To someone who turned me away, I offered pearls today. I dusted off my shoes, and again I went to pray.

Pretty

He smiled
and said

you look so pretty
when you cry.

Virginity

It's my first time — he explains.
It's mine, too.

Fingers intertwined with my belt loops
He pulls them down with no hesitation.
Sexual frustration and teen angst in a cabin.
I was just bored, didn't realize how it would happen.
No one warns you that the first time is just pain.
It feels like shame — it's a bloody stain on the sheet.
Crying out in agony for him to only hear the sweet,
For him to say, "Could you just hold on a little bit longer?"
Swallowing men's pain has never really made me stronger.

Did you finish?
Yes. Of course, I did.

And for years and for men I just tried and lied.
I thought something was just wrong inside
Until I met one that did what others can't do.
It turns out it was not me, it was you.

Hazing

I found out about it
later.

About how
they were supposed to
record everything.

They listened to it
anyway.

They listened to
his date with me.

Crowded around the recorder
they listened
as I broke down.

They listened to me cry
when he tried to kiss me.

They listened to me
make tearful apologies.

They listened to me
try to explain
what had happened
that I had been raped
a few months before.

They listened to me
chokingly mutter
that I was sorry.
for thinking I was ready to date

for ruining his night.

I found out later
that some of them laughed
as they listened to me
as they listened
to our date.

At the end of which
he was supposed to have sex
with me
and secretly record it
for them all to enjoy
a task they had all been given
a way to prove their worthiness
of brotherhood.

Still
they listened.

Crowded around the recorder
in the basement
of the fraternity house.

They listened to me
and they did not get up.

They did not run from the room.
They did not say turn it off.
They did not scream out
I can't listen to this
I can't bear to listen to this.

They listened to me
and they did not cry.
They did not grab the recorder
and smash it against the wall.

They did not pound their strong fists on the floor.
They did not scream out
what is happening to us
what have we become.

I found out later
that some of them apologized
to him for me
for what an awful date I was.

But none of them ever apologized to me
even though
it's true
they saw me
every day.

I like to move

I like to move
It's an opportunity to be someone new
A carefully curated character just for the audience or you
A midwest belle when I flee to the south, a party queen in be-
tween
Morphing like the power rangers I used to adore on the screen

But instead of fighting villains I'm fighting the clock
A high schooler trying to live on my own what a shock
Bills don't pay themselves and I don't have time to rest
Likable is a survival skill when life puts me to the test
And sure you might be stressed with AP anatomy
And sometimes I really wish that life was for me
But I can't think about it now- I have dimes to push
I sold all the bags of grass but I think I have some kush.

Ope- Pack it up
All over again
Everything important in one little box
Remembering that I'm attending the School of Hard Knocks
Then I'm the clueless girl with an uncle moving blues
Felony arrest- he's gone awhile but so's the money too
Grind and push just to get by then quick- pack it up again.
Remember to paint on the smile you gotta look like a friend

Sell my soul to the Navy maybe now I won't stray from water
These men are hitting on me saying I look like their daughter
Cue the pseudo southern lady who couldn't hide her pride
Decisions were less about being smart and more for the ride.

Pack it up now I'm a mama with a nurturing role
The mother wound never happened gotta let it go
She did the best she could with what that she had

And If you want to blame her you better blame dad
And if you blame them better blame their parents too
And don't forget about the trauma that wasn't passed to you

Pack it up- be professional there's no time to feel
We've got project deadlines hurry up you gotta heal
Don't let these people know who you are
Hide all the bad, the immense internal scar

But where did I pack it- my ability to be real?
Where was the skin that I felt comfortable inside?
Where is the person I kept trying to hide?

Who

Me.

Myself squarely agreeing with you. Seeking your praises and pleasing too. I want your approval, scavenging for love. Is it me? I don't know, is your smile for me or for you? I can't tell who agreed. Is it fake me, or real me/you?

The me inside was not asked. Me does not matter, I do not pass. Was that me, doing what you wanted me to do? I said the words you liked to hear. I went to the places you wanted me to steer. Me? No, I don't matter. Whatever you want to do. Who's me? There is no me. Myself is too selfish to choose, say, or do.

Can I only be me when I'm alone, so I can't feel the presence of the unknown. No one, not anyone else around? Others plead needing, wanting, controlling, waiting for me. When I am alone, I get to be me. Lonely, empty, nothing. Selfish now for being alone and lonely, until there is no self.

I call you and ask what you need, how are you, and how can I help? Can I start to grow a little and be fed? What lives between my belly and my head? Grow to say, "no", "no, thank you", and 'I'd like to do this, or that."

Me grows with each no, no, no, no's. No's line up, soldiers form long platinum chains. A shiny new spine aligns and rings. Hardened bones of strength uphold. A neck to look around and support my growth. Swiveling eyes go left and right, taking in all the sights. I see you, but you see me too? Am I here now?

Me, myself, and I, with you. You, yourself, being you with me taking turns, us being two. Abandon praise seeking, approval waiting or begging for love. No taking. Not over-giving, too much. No lying. No longer a hole, I'm whole. You and me, not broken or pieces, whole selves together.

We.

Picture perfect

Going through these pictures
I wonder how I smiled so much
I knew what I was experiencing
They knew, too

Those people behind the camera
Expecting my smile, demanding my good girl performance
And I perform
A desperate bid for connection
To belong

I smile and I flirt with the camera
I'm such a good girl
Love me, just love me, please
I can smile, I can be a good girl
They smile, too, seemingly proud of my performance

Then the camera is gone
The moment of deception over
No connection
No belonging

But I'm such a good girl, and no one sees me.

Un-cluttering

Ah-choo! In the attic, my fingers leave five dusty scars across a box of hoarded memories. Here again and looking for the same. What? Things to throw away, of course. Surrounded by blue, orange, and fleur de lis boxes; some black, some white. Stacks of vessels, painted, decorated, bursting with painful powers. I am looking for something. What, again? Oh, yeah, pain to throw away.

The goal: to pitch one item. Period. Even just a single photo. Naw, I could do more. How about I toss a whole box today? No, two! But better yet… what if I could dump the entire shrine of these dusty remains? All of it!? I can do it. I will get the biggest black garbage bag I can find and fill it to capacity with this excrement. I'll go now, in a minute. Yes, this can be quick and painless.

A contemplating finger slips under the lid as I rise. What about the good memories? The thought sprouts in my brain. No, pluck that. I should do it without even looking inside. There weren't any good memories. Cast the past all at once. My fresh start. But… if I find some pictures I want to keep, that would be worth just a few minutes of looking… right? This box. So heavy. Maybe the softball trophy is in here. "Undefeated," it said, and my brain tempts. So I'll only check this box. I tip the top.

Pandora slaps hard and cold. Stacks of photos' colored corners whack me. "Weak." "Stupid." "Loser," they attack. Why did I look? What was I looking for again? Cruel time machine revs her engine and we take off, traveling light years in a second. I am back there. I brought myself here, stupid. My fault. *No, thank you, I am just looking,* I want to say to the peddling pain. Bargaining for anything salvageable in this decade. I'll order things to throw away. Hold on to me. Hold my breath and pray. I can't breathe the air in this decade. Grab it and get out! This one? This photo? My fingers stick, glued to the heavy pic before I can think.

My dog. I loved her, the one she called "the neighborhood whore." Maggie Mae, she must've had nine litters of puppies to sell. Nine times nine equals 81 puppies. I held them all. Born out of tangles with neighborhood stags. Here's one: our family, back when we were a family. Here's one: There's me. Little. Dirty. Ugly. Smiling. Why the hell was I smiling? What year was this? This, that, then, now, a time from a place who knows no time, a time when he stayed. He's still here, staying still. This one. Him. Big. Dirty. Ugly. Smiling. Welcomed in. They all knew who he was... allowed him in anyway. "Stay out," I said, and he did. Whew. I won, but the other girls he hurt. He won't hurt me, but I didn't protect the others. Me. Big. Angry, bitter, cold girl, strong only for me. I couldn't protect the others. This one. Me, hands on hips. Get out! Be afraid of me: I'll tell! The one, her drunk, I told. Her — she guzzled a whole bottle of *I don't care*. This one, drinking, stoned, laughing and why is he, was he, there again, uh, I mean, here?

Now, then, in our nightmares. Another sharpened photo slices. This one, little girls pleasing, smiling, hurting. My guard was only down for a minute. Trust no one, a truth I knew too well.

Little girls, no more playing, buried smiling. Can't trust then or now, guards up! Don't sleep. Stay sharp. Little girls, things to throw away. Weakened hands, the dusty box slips. It cuts. Out spills hurt on the floor, untangling my guts in rows of ribbons for tightly wrapping wounds. I shove my contents back in. Pack it up. Re-seal the tomb, a flimsy cardboard lid. Closed. Little mummified girls never to be seen again.

Replaced dust, resealed secrets entombed.

Contingency

I found things while packing up.
I found her passports. Why didn't we talk about her trip to Japan?
She was so young.
She never would have gone out with the back of her hair like that
    or with those socks. I want to hear about her trips.
I found all the backups of toothpaste, gauze, moisturizer, apple-
    sauce, etc., etc. so she'd never have to fear running out. Were
    all her backups in the way of us talking about her trip to
    Japan?
Why was it always uncomfortable? Was I tripping over toothpaste
    and moisturizer to try to reach her?
I found boxes and boxes of every card and letter saved. She held
    on. She wanted connection. I believe she did.
Maybe the fear of the fear of not enough......dental floss, graham
    crackers.......was holding so tight
that there was no getting in and no coming out.
Holding so tight she bypassed just holding. She hugged so tight
    she went right past the point of together.

A time when I struggled to make a decision

Before I even get out of bed, I can't decide. To get more
    much-needed sleep, or get up early to work out, write, or vis-
    it over coffee with family and friends.
Work will begin soon, but I can't decide. The decision: to do what
    I ought or do what they want? I go in the direction of need,
    called away to serve and do what I am supposed to do. To
    get praise, to do what I get noticed when I do.
Push myself in each direction all at once. Please, support and
    make certain they all feel loved. Running in circles, I run out
    of gas, until I ought to go to bed or
Ought to stay up and practice, or write, or clean, or take care of
    my awful nails and skin so I look good for them. Who's
    them? Am I needed again? Here I am for the tears or fears
    or bedtime talks for the family. It's a privilege to give, I
    would not trade it.
Tomorrow I will decide to claim those things calling me to create
    them, make them, and learn those skills. Did I decide or did
    I just fall asleep?

Facing the past

I knew it would never be the same
Could never be what I pretended it had been.
I could not go back to the past,
especially a past that never existed.

I longed for a dream,
I longed for an un-reality,
A place where I was loved & protected,
A place where I belonged.

I knew that no amount of pretending would make it real.
I knew that my falsehoods
Created in a desperate bid to protect my child self, would fail.
I knew & I went back anyhow,
Facing truths I spent a lifetime burying.

I acknowledged the chasm
Between make-believe & reality,
The one I would have to bridge.

Many things were the same —
The house, the trees, the roads —
Except now they were only bare bones
Holding neither the pain I was afraid of
Nor me captive to something that never existed.

I was freed

No longer afraid to acknowledge reality,
No longer held in stasis
By self-augmented memories of something yearned for —
yet utterly false.

The grief as old as me
No longer clawing at me day after day,
Begging me not to deny its existence.
An old grief, now an old friend
With softer, well worn edges.

les fleurs d'hiver

As I turned back toward the river,
Blinking at the frost settling in along the edge of my lashes,
I stopped to linger at the field of dead flowers,
Their delicate browned stalks casting shadows against the
      fresh-fallen snow,
Formerly soft petals now frozen in atrophy,
Curved heads bowed in repose,
A stark reminder that summer had once been here, too.

SUSAN

Bridge

A bridge that sometimes goes beyond
A bridge that sometimes brings me back, to me, generational me,
    so that I can feel that there is somewhere I belong.
Other stories, people, events are not where I belong. I may feel
    connected, momentarily home
but betrayal is possible, disappointment is part of the deal.
Horton hears a who and we are but a speck, yet within each speck
    is the cosmos and legacy.
We want to make sense of it, we try even if it holds fallacy.
Striving to feel belonging, I cross the bridge not to get to the
    other side, but to get to know the bridge.

On yearning

I want to go back
To do it all over again
Starting the first night at the restaurant
The heavy velvet curtains
The way he slipped his hand into mine
Leaned over and kissed my cheek
And later on up on the rooftop
A bottle of wine and the cool fall air
With my dog, and the glow of Manhattan.

I want to go back to that first night he stayed with me
I told him I needed to sleep
He said he never slept
I made us coffee in the morning
I still have the shirt he had been wearing that night
The one I pulled onto my own body that morning
It's still on the bent metal hanger, wrapped in plastic
from the cleaners down the street.

I want to go back to my first trip to Utah
To feel the excitement
To not be exhausted
To not be afraid
To not feel the shock
Heavy in my body like so many stones.

I want to go back to Central Park
To run and feel my strong legs carry me away
To marvel at the vast quiet spaces hidden in the city
The get lost in the bramble
To feel him slip his arms around
And pull me in for a kiss.

I want to go back
All the way back
To those days
In the beforetime
When I had him inside of me
When we were together always
Inseparable
A single breath.

I want to go back
To the time when I didn't know
When I wouldn't have been able to imagine
The things that I now know.

I want to go back
To when Mom was still alive
And I wasn't yet an orphan or a mother
But just a daughter
Just a girl.

I want to go back
To be able to choose
To know that this is this and that is that
and to say yes I want this not that
I want it to be different
I want to be different.

I told her last week that I hadn't felt myself since Mom died
That I hadn't been the same
How could I be the same after all?
One day I had a mother
And then I had a box of ashes
And myself
Of course, I had myself
And I still had him
I still had them

But now everything was different.

Pruning

In between invitation and ocean, a vastness
She did not go
Corn and corn and rows of late summer heat
The blooms grow wild and unabashed
The red bud takes one long last grasp at growing
It will be ripped from the root.
He dreads the dismembering, whatever grows should stay.
Whatever grows should not go.
Whatever wild, unruly, and eager life that is there, should be let to live.
It sends deep the root, spreads wide the stalk.
The garden grows green, then grey.
She will not stay.

Lovesong

Bring to me your pain, love
With its knives and blood
Its rage and terror
And relentless hunger to devour.

Bring to me your fear, love
Set it down on my delicate flesh
Pour it into my still fragile body
Whisper it into my breath.

Bring to me your wound, love
Tear it out of yourself
As if it had not always been there
As if it had not festered and taken hold.

Bring to me your sorrow, love
Lift it up from your deepest parts
Imagine that it could be contained
And that I might be able to hold it just so.

Bring to me your hopes, love
Because I promised you could
Because I wanted to share them
Because I promised I would.

Bring to me your truth, love
With its aching regret
All of the hallowed out places
That I now know I cannot ever possibly fill.

Hand to self

Untethered from my self
Down to the cave of shame and isolation
There is no one who will take my hand
The confusion of family
The humanity of tilling our ground
Tired,
My hand to self is rest and quiet.

The haunting hours

I leaned over and fumbled for the clock
Wondering whether it was morning yet
Checking the big window for any light peeking through
Knowing that sometimes
And especially these days
The way the snow throws up the moon's shine
can easily mimic the dawn.

I decided instead
To just breathe
Knowing as I did
That this would calm me down
And place me where I was
Safely in my own bed
Awake and alert
Once again
In the haunting hours.

That night I had been asleep
My son stretched out alongside me
Smelling of the creek and the forest
And the promises of spring.

I hadn't been afraid that night
I hadn't even known about him
I hadn't seen his face yet
Or the confidence in the set of his jaw
as he walked about in the dark.

It had been overcast and rainy for days
And when the sun finally rose in its early morning brilliance
It lit up the row of windows overlooking the pond
I screamed in terror at the line of smeared handprints

Now visible at the very center of each otherwise
perfectly clean window.

And then, of course, there were the scant, smudged
glove marks in the bedroom
And the muddied footprint at the edge of the window well
Where he lost his footing and slipped
As he reached over to test the sash.

The police were no help
Not at first anyway
And then afterwards, when I called again later,
I knew I could never call them again.

I hadn't been afraid that night
The fear came for me later
After he had already left
When I knew he'd been there
When I understood that he'd been hunting me
All those months
Watching
Waiting
Learning
Getting to know my dog.

There were the beer cans near the shed
that I had assumed were the painters'
The night sensor that had stopped working
The small hole in the fence
The feeling I had every time I walked past the tall yellow waders
The ones that had remained hanging untouched all those months
On a single hook in the wall
Just next to the door in the basement.

When we finally packed up to move,
I found the hole that he had cut
Hidden as it had been all of that time
Just behind the waders.

3:33am

Wake up heart-crazed
To get out of this cage
I don't know why — but I want to run
I've got to leave now — under the gun.

Danger just has to be near
It hurts too bad
I feel too sad
A push to be here
A pull to be there.

I just need to sprint
I don't really know where
I don't really know why
Maybe because a decade ago I ran into this guy —
Now I don't feel safe anymore.

Still 3 a.m. silence captures me back
Go to sleep fine, wake up under attack
Ready to fight, but there's no one there but me
Wash, rinse, repeat, wait, and work to be free.

See unspeakable horrors, then go to work
Do box breathing so I'm not going berserk
Every conversation to humor I'm gliding
No silence allowed in this high I am riding.

Don't want to hear my own thoughts
I need noise and love and laughter
A reminder that life can be okay after.

Today I see

Over the years I have thought that the "greatest" crime was that he
    stole my body, my innocence.
He stole spirit, safety, trust, sexuality.
Today I see that he stole love.

Mad

What??!!??

"Why didn't you scream or tell?"

WHAT?????
Why didn't he stop?
Why did he keep drinking?
Why did he keep coming home?
Why did he rape me?
Why didn't he get help?

Sometimes I get so mad. When our stories remain in silence and
        shame, we do not heal, connect, empower
Their power thrives in the dark, in the silence and shame. I speak
        for all the others.
Sometimes I get so mad. My anger feels like a call to action.
The energy of anger moves me to speak

It is not okay.
This is not okay.
Our bodies, our children.

I am the one who has no family. I did years of therapy and
        healing work.
I am the one who struggles with my body, my sexuality,
        trust, safety.

I do not want to be where they are, but I am mad.

Mama bear

That unpredictable black bear they fear,
Her murderous claws and wide jaw,
Ready to snap.
Take a look, a wide open view adorned with pointed teeth,
So sharp they'll puncture every part of you, man.
Erect ears, a pointed warning,
Musky fur stands electric.
Flames reflect in eyes that warn, stay back —
That mama bear,
That's me.
I spend the days fiercely protecting and teaching my offspring.
Training my cubs to live in the wild world they will oversee.
Training my young lady cubs:
Be untouchable by any predator, man or boy.
Raising skilled protectors
Alert to sight or smell any scent of prey.
Aware of danger, they will pounce first, instill fear, remain
        untouched
Unharmed as the weaker species slinks away.
Until they are grown,
And it's their turn to train their babies
Sharpening the next generation to sense, warn, and annihilate
        all threats.
We won't be prey again.

A voice restored

My secret was trying to kill me. I kept my story hidden deep inside the tapestry of my soul, which had the power to suffocate me. Or, liberate me once and for all. Sure, I lived through the silence and darkness— battling, loving, thriving, coping never realizing that the secret of what happened to me that night affected every part of my existence, like an anchor to a boat. The weight of my secret bore down on my spirit, dragging me down into its unforgiving depths. Constantly threatening to drown me once and for all.

Followed by the rapid progression of things falling apart. Failing health. Failing relationships. Failing everything. But when I opened my heart to God and the universe, I found the most amazing husband, yet I still somehow, could not bear to share everything that had been stolen from me so many years ago.

Until one ordinary day 35 years later when I overheard the story of another survivor on the news and the words TRAIN RAPES echoed like an impending storm. While standing at my kitchen sink, the word train still reverberating loudly in the corridors of my mind, I could see her there: the 17-year-old girl who was once me, standing disheveled, clutching only one shoe. I could see the panic and shame in her eyes, looking at me as though she were waiting for me to finally stand up for her. So, with wet, soapy hands and a dishtowel draped over my shoulder, I shouted to my husband, the words I never thought I'd utter: "That is what happened to me!"

Suddenly, I felt free. And loved. With each passing day, I have emerged from the depths of my own darkness, untethered and alive.

On knowing

In the beginning I knew
From the dark pools in his eyes
That he knew what I knew
About suffering inside.

And he saw that I knew
From the blue shine in my eyes
That sometimes just love
Can make it all right.

And I knew
What I knew
That he loved me
So much.

And he knew
What he knew
That he loved me
Too much.

And he knew
That I did not know
The demons
He fought.

Until one day
I knew what it meant
To know
Nothing at all.

SUSAN

I am a daughter

My relationship with my mom has been changing since she died. She was alone, in the hospital, with COVID. I wish I had been able to be there with her; I wish I could have said goodbye. I wish we had more time to talk.

We've had a difficult relationship. It wasn't easy, but she stuck around (we both did) for the hard conversations and feelings we needed to have to try to work towards understanding and repair. I miss her in the small moments, like when I was wondering if Jack's Drugs was called Jack's Drugs, and I thought to call and ask her.

I feel her presence in a different way now. I appreciate that. Her presence is more comfortable for me. I feel open and warm. I have compassion for her struggle. When she was here, I would get so frustrated that she didn't understand me (she told me so: "I never understood you"). I felt agitated and disconnected. She didn't protect me.

I wrote her a note when I was in my 20's:

> Mom,
> Irwin was the Nazis, and you were the United States.
> Me

It seemed she could not go to the place in her that would have helped her empathize with what happened to me or for her to truly apologize. I saw her limits, but they hurt me and caused me harm.

But no matter, mom loss is a singular experience. It feels deep and earthy. It feels boundless and nebulous, cosmic that is. To be of her body and then that body is gone. The soul cord remains.

Pin me to the lattice

Pin me to the lattice
That I might not fall again today
That I might feel the sun touch all of the places
Long hidden from its rays.

Pin me to the lattice
That I might be able to stretch out just so
That I might feel my legs unfurl from their place
against my chest
My arms reaching out as if in an embrace.

Pin me to the lattice
That I might lift my face up to the sky
So that my eyes might open wide
So blue and bright and true.

Pin me to the lattice
That its lovely patterns might be able to sustain me
That all of those delicate x's
Might recognize my plight.

Pin me to the lattice
That I might feel its reinforcements
That with it I might grow back together the broken parts
So I no longer have to stand in this body all alone.

Quitting perseverance

The hardest calls to make are the calls not returned by the police department.

"Hi, just checking for any updates on my case. Please call me— BEEP!"

If I am happy with my message, I am supposed to press 1. So I stand, weak-kneed, and I press 1. I wait. Ticking away the tocks, hot summer days go by as my temperature rises. Then the weekend comes. Sat and Sun come and go. The cyclical silent treatment from the investigating detective brings me down. Persistent darkness and sadness haunt me when no one calls back. Why should I care? The summer fades, and I remember to forget to call again.

Fall comes. I find myself weakened like leaves, on my knees and praying. Rising only to climb into bed where I shudder and hide under the covers from others. The little light left in my heart catches fire from the wind outside. Anger helps me spring back again. I pay for every ounce of energy with a pound of acidic rage, flowing inside, and burning my pride. Boiling over to overflowing, I sense hate leaking outside of me.

Okay, I'll call again.

"Hi! Me… again. If you have any updates on my case, please call — BEEP"

If I am happy with my message, I am supposed to press 1. I smash one. I smash so hard the key might break. One! I pray. The leaves fall and no one returns my call.

I'm slipping underneath. Winter layers on his hard hits, piling the cold onto my body. The white, snowy days highlighting and hiding my powerlessness. Columns of ice sharpen, slicing and cutting my pain over and over again.

I drive far. Not to wreck, but to get away. "Never give up," explodes on a bus stop ad for sneakers. I drive by and laugh out loud, "never!?" But the light is lit, and my gray matter swiftly kicks my feelings again. Throwing good sense out the window and leaving brains on the side of the road. An idea allows a brief injection of fuel, it sparks. "I can do it", enough of a catalyst to throw good energy back into the black hole again. Hey, this time I'll send cookies, or doughnuts. Cops love those. So I send chocolate, and a nice, well-written note that would make a grandma proud.

I write, "Just checking in! I wanted to thank you for working on my case. Please let me know if there are any updates."

Silence. Darkness turns in, towards me. I rightly suspect I don't matter. The verdict is — there will be no verdict. Maybe it wasn't that big of a deal. Is there evidence that people get raped by home intruders all the time? Maybe it's the standard order of operations? Justice served; maybe I deserved it. Plot twist, maybe the cops are bad and...? Maybe I should, nope — no one cares. They are just too busy. Someone was probably murdered since, or maybe... even... raped? I can't stand this thought; I shake my head at that thought. But it grows. What if he is still out there, and I could have stopped him from doing it again?

Buds are on the tree. Already? I close the curtains, I will ignore spring, annoying on her way. But those buds lived and reemerged, so can I. I crawl to the phone. In a moment of weakness, the rebirth of a world outside my window inspires. I will try to try again.

"Mr. Detective, This is Ginger. My case file is...."

I hang up. No words. I write another email reminding the detective that I am waiting, but I delete it. I will simmer on high, boiling in my own bones. Mopping, sweeping, it is so hard to move it all away. Blasting anger outward but returning to myself. Stewing in injustice juice, hoping none lands on those I love most. Be quiet. Stop. Don't call, don't do it. Be still and know He is God. Justice is His.

Quietness comes and stays.

No one wants to hear a story about a serial rapist who never got caught.

My ritual

My need to prepare.

It takes me closer —
a way to get out the door,
feeling inner confidence to begin the day,
gathering all that is important,
especially my shoes.

We all know great despair in a lost shoe.

I scour my closet for the next day's outfit and I feel happy —
knowing and seeing a colorful picture,
a rough draft before my slumber —
hopeful upon sunrise and morning's breath,
the aroma of coffee will fill my senses
as I head towards the door.

Peak seeking

My path meanders again and again
No one has been this way before
No trail to follow
Brush is thick
Slashes write red across my limbs
I go on.
Sweaty fear stinks, my heart thumps, thumping cries
Uh oh, you should be afraid, beats the muscle drum in my chest

I have no idea where I am
Footprintless, untraveled land
A glance back to where I have been
NO
Those paths are not for me
I blaze on

I reign dominion over the bushes
Get out of my way
Make my mark on the route
Scrape my feet on the soil
I leave a new trail
My tribe has not traveled this lane
but my followers will
No, I say, to ancestral ideas that pop
No thanks, go away
I go on

Each day newer than the last
Never familiar or comfortable
An adventure in trusting God and myself
Reach the top
Ahhh, the view is amazing
Ocean and rivers and life all around

Flourishing goes up, not down
Distance reveals another peak
It calls me to seek
I'll go up that way as well.

Sun/Rain

I searched for you in the sun.
It always felt like that was your home.

Golden rays would bounce off you —
No matter if you were alone —
It was a perfect hue.

Surface layers happy thoughts and giggles.
But now it's just a memory passed,
It was fun, but it would not last.

Now — I search for you in the rain.
I no longer have to hide from hardship
There is a beauty in the realism of pain
A badge of honor in honesty.

And even when it's killing me,
I know that I will persevere
Because I know that I was born to be here.

So I will say goodbye to the sun.
Sure, she was fun, but the rain —
The rain keeps me sane.

In the forest where the deer sleep

There is a solemn quietness in the forest
that feels almost as if sound had ceased to exist
With all its stately old trees in various states
of nearly perfect disarray
The old cedar showcasing its stacked rooms
with views onto the water
Exposed roots intertwined so tightly with rocks
that they had no choice but to topple together.

Underneath the pine boughs we can see
great depressions in the snow
Large elegant contours where the deer laid down to rest
Now decorated with a spattering of needles matted
into the otherwise pristine white cover
Their delicate tracks leading to and fro like so many pairs
of hearts crisscrossing the forest floor.

Sometimes in the late afternoons we venture there together
To run and pray and breathe in the trees
And marvel at the light brightening the very tops of the tall birch
And stop to rest on the large rock propped up by a vast tangle
of roots hidden just beneath the snow.

Haiku.2

The moon & I have
a true thing with each other
water, pull, and love.

At the hemlock

On the banks of the river
Down where the cattails are thick with water
And no path has been cut
There stands an old hemlock tree.

I find her quiet beauty a comfort
Her long limbs stretched out just so
Parts of her roots peeking out like feet in the tall grass
Her massive trunk too large to encircle with my own small arms.

Long ago, someone nailed a piece of wood into her side
There's just a small part left now
The nails' metal heads turned orange with rust
As if they had something important to say.

And then there is the scorched part of her
Near the base, facing the river
Her bark charred with black ash as if it were coal.

Strewn about her there is rebar
Abandoned campfires
Discolored beer cans
The remains of an old rug.

And, of course,
there is me.

Again

The road map of yesterday embedded in my soul
Taking up the spaces where I want the future to grow

Slipping through the cracks of the past
Finding secret passages to tomorrow

I imagine tsunamis that wipe it all away
Floods that nourish the desolation
Gentle rains to settle the dust

My heart blazing a new path
I am a child again.

Pashut Tofi'u

It's an ongoing struggle, a persistent effort
to allow safety when it is available
To not always be gearing up for the horrible and scary
To rest in ease and play
Yet then we talk of the reality of the dangers all around,
not the old ones,
not the known ones,
the lurking, waiting, licking their lips ones
I remember it is a daredevil move
To breathe, to let my shoulders down
and trust in the moment
or another
or in something
To put down the knife or the scream
But nature shows me the beauty of a persistent spring
in spite of the humans licking their lips
It shows up
So do we.

Over now

People sometimes ask:
Will you ever get over it?

It is not so much that they are waiting for this —

(For me
to get over it)

(How long ago did it happen now?)

It is rather that they want to believe
That they have to believe
(please, god, let it be true)
that one can get over it.

Just in case
it should happen to them
(please, god, let it be over now)
just in case it should happen
to their daughter
their partner
their wife
their mother sister brother
friend
child.

Just in case it should happen to them
(please, god, let it be over)
They ask
because they want to believe
that one can get over it
(please, god, let it be true)
striking so randomly

as it does

any time
(day or night)

anywhere
(in the alley
on the train
at the bus stop
in the stairway
the bedroom
the hallway)

without the least discrimination
(black white yellow brown
young old
man woman)

caring about nothing
relentlessly devouring everything in its wake
(please, god, let it be over now)
they ask because
they want to believe
they have to believe
(please, god, let it be true)
that one can get over being raped.
(please, god, let it be true).

Wants

I want
I want you to hear me
I want you to see me
I want you to understand what I don't even understand
Then, I want you to explain it to me

I want to know why I wasn't seen
I want to know why I wasn't heard
I want things I can never have
I want things I was cheated out of
I want so much and yet when asked,
"What do you want?" I have no answers

I want to have an answer
I want my experiences to have meaning
I want my existence to have purpose

I want things we never talk about
I want the thing we barely speak
in whispers to ourselves
I want it all.

Thought experiment

Try this:

Imagine
a world
where rape
was as despised
as deplorable
contemptible
unacceptable
as morally reprehensible
as lynching.

Imagine
a day
where violence
against women
was repugnant
rather than
ordinary

was tragic
catastrophic
and heartbreaking
rather than
entertaining.

Where women
were no longer
bought and sold
like so much chattel.

Were no longer
just

so many
rented holes.

And now:
try it at home.

Try it in the morning
over coffee
with toast.

Try it at the office
in the boardroom
the classroom.

Try it in the emergency room
and the courtroom.

Try it in the nightclub
try in the bathroom
and the coatroom.

Try it at the bar
and the table.
Try it over dessert.

Try it
in the evening
before bed
with your partner
your spouse
your children
and grandchildren.

Try it on the bus
the train
the plane.

Try it in the alley.
Try it in your car.

Try it in the gym
on the playground
the football field
the basketball court.

Try it at church.

Try it everywhere
the implicit endorsement
of violence against women
is allowed to lurk.

As the light heals

As the light enters my body through the cracks of past pains,
I feel a healing sensation that I've never experienced before.
A warm sensation washes over me, and I begin to feel
the chains of despair release the hold they've had on me.
I experience freedom through the light from the prison in my
    mind
that I've held onto all of these years, releasing me from the
    captivity of sorrow.
As the light continues to wash through my body,
the sorrow I once felt is replaced with joy and hope.

Summertime

Reflecting on my teenage years, I couldn't help but feel a profound sense of emptiness. My memories seemed mired in mistakes, lost chances, and the nightmare of a tragedy my senior year of high school — a period in my life characterized by confusion and self-doubt. As the years passed, my old friends' faces and laughter erased from my mind, yet a sense of belonging clung to my heart like a worn-out glove.

Until one day, a message appeared — conversations ensued. Then a spark of joy ignited at thoughts of an invitation to meet, knowing it could mean a chance to reclaim moments of our past and gain insight into each other's years gone by. After much contemplation, I chose to go.

We realized that the one great love of any teenager was the smell of summer. At 52, we found ways to break away from reality and made our way to the beach. We rekindled old times and shared stories of our lives — the many storms we have weathered, the losses endured along the way, and times of great success and happiness — the sun's heat blanketing us with warmth and hope. The saltiness of the ocean breeze gave way to peace and serenity amid a sea of uncertainty.

On the way home, the sun beaming down on my car, I couldn't help but feel like me again.

Monday morning at the woodpile

The wood had become heavy by then
Having sat all piled up together since just after the last snowfall.
That morning, the branches and sticks had soaked up
some of the night's rain.
With my dog beside me, I looked around
for a pair of trees to hold the wood.

That first stack was tall and elegant,
Held as it was between two strong birches.
Modest though they were,
They seemed to welcome their new load.

The dog was busy with the squirrels in their usual game,
Their shrill chirps piercing the air as she threatened
from the bottom of the tree
I lifted a pair of logs into my gloved hands,
Remembering how the fingertips of the suede
had been burned through during the winter.
I carried the logs to the trees and placed them
against each other just so,
Log by log, piece by piece,
listening for the gentle sound of the wood
nestling in its new place as I set them down.

When it was finally time to gather up the remnants
of the morning's big pile,
I turned to see the sun beaming through the stacks,
Casting gentle rays of light through perfectly imperfect
gaps in the stacks held together by the trees,
And I wondered at the marvelous wood that would
keep me warm all winter
Now transformed into some kind of rustic art
at home here in the forest.

I brushed at the log debris covering my arms
Noted the fresh red scratches from the berry bushes
Ran my right hand through my spiderwebbed hair
And thought about just how much of a lifetime away
that night in Los Angeles was from me now.

Connected

You know that feeling
When you stand barefoot on the beach toes buried deep
Each wave shifting the sand beneath your feet
Pulling
Shifting

And you shift, too
Dancing with each wave

I can feel it in my whole body
The shifting dance of life
Swaying with forces that could knock me down
Yet I still stand
Wave after wave
Shifting, shifting
Dancing, dancing

In the liminal spaces, again

The trip I took with my brother after college
That one is stored in my hair
The scent of the mint shampoo as the outdoor shower washed it
      down my body
Smelling it even now brings me back to that spring in Jerusalem.

I had almost forgotten about the modest blue shirt hanging in my
      closet
Nearly crowded out by the French clothes I bought for work
It is where the memories of sleeping on the couch in her hospital
      room are stored
It was just starting to get cool outside, and I needed the long
      sleeves
How strange that my beautiful sister did not outlast this simple
      cotton shirt.

My mother is stored deep inside me
As if I had carried her in my very body
As if she had lived there for all those years
I felt her today as a hawk flew overhead
What I wouldn't give for another day with her.

And Lizzy
It's not really that she is stored somewhere, but that we are
For her, I exist in the water
In the lake where she died
It is where our memories are
If it is even possible to store memories that you never even
      really had.

My son cannot be contained
Cannot be stored
But he is saved in every cell of my body
I look at him and see that he also carries me with him
I am stored in his eyes
His skin
His strong jaw
His sharp words
The ease with which he moves his body
And the certainty we share about the depth of our love for
        each other
Something that scares us both.

Sometimes I imagine that I am a magical vessel
That I am able to carry things too heavy for my human body
Things that are too hard or elusive to pick up
Things that cannot be grasped
That cannot be forgotten
Things like the river, and the air
And moonlight and songs
And, of course, love.

I have always known

Before words, I built it
Only I can fit
No one can get to me there
I am alone but
I am preserved and
When the time came,
I emerged, determined
To find my voice,
my choices,
my self.
I refused to live as an expression of their denied pain
Or as a reaction to their actions.
I have always known.
I was willing to go back there to bring her back,
To show her safety, love, play.
From there, I see what is possible
I see compassion
I see my mission: to live from wholeness and integrity.

In this my heavenly body

In this my heavenly body
I know that I am whole
(Which seems impossible somehow
After everything that's happened.)

I wish I could go back in time now
To feel once again all the almost-forgotten days
A little girl camping under the big skies out west
A teenager teetering along the shore of the beach at night
That night with my husband on the roof
The one when we had just met.

In this my heavenly body
There was a night when blood was shed
IVs were placed
A bandage over cotton on my arm
They told me to take care
That is wasn't my fault
That she wouldn't have made it after all.

In this my heavenly body
I breathe the deep scents of the forest
My eyes marvel that the hemlock needles are the very shade of my hair
And my eyes the very color of the water
Exactly when we are both bathed in the sun.

In this my heavenly body
My mouth has learned to speak truths
To combat the fears stalking my mind
To channel the rage welling up in my heart
To say no — you cannot do that.

In this my heavenly body
I grew a boy.

Swallowing lilies

Swallowing lilies, we left the dirty south behind
And passed our last cigarette between hand to hand
lips parted laugh
tobaccoed tongue
smoothing down gullet and gall.

Sun weary- travel torn and tired
she cut her hair out the open window
clumsy cuts with dull blades
her waist length tresses
chipped away, like ax to live oak
ash blonde billowed away in clumped clouds
we wound our way north west, Florida, Georgia and now Tennessee.

Our dog slept silent,
quiet, content
paws folded with feathered fur across the contents of our
cramped car
candied dresses, cat gut strings.

That dog- long since gone
given back to a love - long since left
and her hair, once shorn, grows again
hung tresses down her strong slender back
once heavy in the sticky south,
warm, now, in endless winter
all, now, a mottled memory.

Light comes late, leaves early
painting pavement and palomino snow.

In the afterwards

Sometimes, in the afterwards

I feel the sun warming my arms
And am grateful for its heat
I marvel at the river bed
With its remnants of long toppled trees
and their still-new growth
I listen to the birds sing
And the woodpecker drumming
his long beak into a tree

I am reminded of my friend Harry's words about enchantment
How once it comes, it somehow stays with a place
At least sometimes
And I notice that I feel alive
The shift in my breathing
The small trail of sand from my son's feet

In the sacred spaces
In the afterwards
When the light penetrates the broken parts
I can feel my very soul exhale
Somewhere behind my ribs and in the back of my throat

And I know that the darkness is only temporary.

Amazing grace

I traced my finger over your tattoos
Focused, I had to remember everything
Warm skin, pores, that rough patch on your arm
A moment to which I forever cling.

Caressing your hair, sweaty and thick
"It's going to be OK. Don't be afraid. We are here."
I would cross oceans, do anything, no price too high
But I can do little more than shed a tear.

I burn into memory the shape of your hands
You have always had such big hands —
the world to hold.

The morphine starts and the breathing slows

We start to sing as the lines smooth
A chest once gasping now struggles to move

"Amazing grace," we sing, and how sweet the sound
Family does not have to be lost to be found.

Music

Bob Marley once said that when it hits you, you feel no pain. I've found this to be true. It moves through my body with a positive vibration that gives any pain I'm experiencing a way to exit my extremities. From one note to the next, I feel my body release the sorrow that once was, turning it into a calming feeling that can only be described with the movement of my hips, the movement of my arms, even the movement of my toes. It's as though the notes are strumming each part of my body, and with each strum, a healing like no other replaces what once was an undesirable feeling. A sense of peacefulness and calm washes over my entire being, and I'm left with the happiness that I have longed for. I give thanks to each instrument, each vocality that strums away my pain that I've been so desperate to relieve. Yes, Bob Marley, you are right. Indeed, when it hits you, you feel no more pain. You are left with peace and calmness that no other drug can give.

Nature

On a spring day, following an intense counseling session, my therapist suggested I take a moment and sit outside to find grounding and solace. As I approached a bench, I was so moved by the enduring strength of a magnificent 400-year-old cypress tree standing so tall and majestic, its branches outstretched like open arms, covering the yard with a giant embrace.

I sat down, marveling at the expansive roots at the base of the tree. These roots stood as a testament to life's enduring challenges. It had witnessed countless storms, yet it continued to thrive and offer shelter to those in need.

Feeling overwhelmed and vulnerable from therapy, a cathartic sob escaped me when a gentle presence caught my attention — an elderly lady standing as resolute and unwavering as the tree itself. She offered no judgment or imposition in her demeanor, and for a brief moment, we exchanged comforting glances. She smiled softly, gently waved, and turned away. Her acknowledgement of my pain filled me with hope and comfort.

As I stood to leave, it was in that moment that I realized that no matter how challenging our lives become, we are never truly alone.

In my body

I could feel

my breath
the air
rushing in
and out
of my lungs
steadily
rhythmically

beads of sweat
lining up
all along my skin
trickling down
my face

my heart
pumping blood
working
to send signals
to send life
throughout
my arms
my legs
my back

my body
I could feel

and for a moment
I thought
perhaps
I will fly away

take these legs
and soar
up into the ethers

give snowflakes a home
inside my mouth
all along the way

raise my arms
up over my head
rejoice

at last
I could feel
my body

as I watched the miles
go by
underfoot
running
so effortlessly now

as if I was just
another part
of the air

I could feel
my breath

and I realized
finally
(at least for this moment)
I had come home.

I am everything

I am everything, holy water and hellfire
There's no hero here, nothing to inspire
Not muse but medusa turning you to stone
Olympian when I need you to leave me alone
I was trapped– see, it was me or it was you
Blackbelt can't match what I've been through
And I don't want you to be scared
I know you think that you came prepared.

But I've studied men that are weak like you
And I know exactly how they act and what they do
Can't control their anger– but just around their women
Only other men seem to cure that raging symptom
Only brave in fights they think they can win
Only challenging her, never challenging him
Changing from Jekyll to Hyde and all in between
But I don't back down when you get mean.

You see, I've been training my whole life for this
So when you throw a punch, I'll duck, you'll miss
I'll take that kick to my back and turn it to power
Inspiration, aspiration, another soul to devour.

Turn battle wounds into stories of glory
To mourn all of those who came before me
Turn my fight response to a career
Planting my feet– I have earned to be here
Men can snarl in my face and now I can laugh
Turn attempts at intimidation into a gaff
Turn all of this pain into healing like water to wine
See, I have been through the fire and came out divine.

Author Biographies

Cary Bach Donahou

Cary Bach Donahou lives in rural Arkansas where she enjoys writing, drawing, and volunteering in her community. She's dedicated to breaking generational cycles of harm, raising her daughters, and advocating for those who are not yet able to advocate for themselves.

Susan Hamin

Susan Hamin is a self-proclaimed non-writer who believes in the power of speaking and writing out loud.

Keena Hildebrand

Keena Hildebrand is a proud wife and mother of three boys. Armed with a bachelor's degree in political science, she delves into the complex systems of social issues, focusing on the pervasive problems of sexual and domestic violence. Since 2016, Keena's passionate advocacy has found a home with the RAINN Speakers Bureau; she recently took her voice to Capitol Hill, urging Congress to add protections for victims of child sexual abuse material.

In addition to her advocacy work, Keena holds another bachelor's degree in occupational safety and health. Her professional journey has taken her into the realms of manufacturing, mining, and construction, where she explores the intricate dynamics between humans and systems. Her focus on understanding and improving these interactions has a direct impact on safety and operational performance. In both advocacy and industry, Keena is dedicated to balancing humanity and organizational dynamics.

Meadow Jones

Meadow Jones received her PhD from the University of Illinois. Her dissertation "Archiving the Trauma Diaspora: Affective Artifacts in the Higher Education Arts Classroom" focused on the use of artistic and material practices in the redress of trauma. In combination with her experience as an AWA facilitator, she has adapted her research and created trauma responsive curriculum and workshops. She is a social practice artist, an award-winning filmmaker, and a community organizer. Her work has been published in literary journals, peer-reviewed scientific journals, poetry collections, books, and chapbooks. She has facilitated arts and writing practices for diverse populations including undergraduates, artists, activists, teachers, teenagers, trauma survivors, prisoners, physicians, and friends. In addition to offering workshops, Meadow provides one-on-one creative consulting and trauma and recovery coaching. In other parts of her life, Meadow is a facilitator at the Gesundheit Institute and the School for Designing a Society, a collaborator with The Prop Theatre, and serves on the Board of Directors of Amherst Writers & Artists.

ANGELA LORE

Angela is a loving wife and mom of two sons and grandmother to two precious grandsons. She was a high school senior when she was taken to a dorm on Tulane University's campus and raped by several football players who invited teammates to watch. After living in shame and secrecy for 35 years, she found the courage to report the crime at the age of 52. While struggling with the concept of justice, Angela found healing as she used her voice and platform to educate others on the effects of sexual violence, especially when alcohol is involved. As a registered nurse, she dedicated her life to compassionate healthcare. Early retirement has allowed her to focus on healing and family. She is learning to paint and enjoys writing and drinking her favorite tea, Earl Grey Lavender

MECKS MAC

Meeks Mac is a native of Bellingham, WA, and grew up in the National Capital Region portion of the Washington metropolitan area. She works closely with Maryland state legislators in efforts to pass mental health initiatives and prison reform bills. She is a member of the RAINN Speakers Bureau and volunteers with her local affiliate NAMI. She is currently pursuing a career in law.

GINGER T. REX

Ginger lives in the fantastic Four Corners area of New Mexico. She is a Christian, a wife, a mom, a film actor, a screenplay writer, an author, and an all-around juggler of jobs. Ginger is a terrible cook but a decent baker. She hates rattlesnakes but enjoys the liveliness of the outdoors. An adventure seeker, she spends time hiking, mountain biking, and skiing with her family. When she's not tending to nine boisterous chickens and three colorful beehives, she keeps her 100-pound dog Renzo-the-Magnificent grinning by taking him on long hikes through the sagebrush and sand of her desert home.

MARY SIMMERLING

Mary is a scholar, poet, and activist who is dedicated to advancing social justice, ending violence, and healing trauma. Her interests include applied ethics, social justice, psychology, trauma recovery, and harnessing the healing powers of the creative self through creative writing and art. Her poem "What I Was Wearing" is the inspiration for thousands of global grassroots art exhibits "What Were You Wearing," that invite survivors to contribute their own stories and representations of the clothing they were wearing when they were assaulted (see more at https://sapec.ku.edu/wwyw). Mary has a diverse yet complementary background in fine art, philosophy, social justice, psychology, and applied ethics. She holds a Ph.D. in philosophy from the University of Illinois at Chicago, where she specialized in applied ethics and social justice. She also holds an MA in psychology from Adler University, where she studied the effects of trauma and the roles of creativity and community in trauma recovery and healing. Mary currently serves as the Senior Research Advisor and as a member of the National Leadership Council for RAINN, and is active in nonprofit organizations in the U.S. and Canada that provide direct services to survivors of trauma. Mary is an affiliate and member of the Board of Directors of Amherst Writers & Artists, and leads writing workshops for survivors of sexual and domestic violence as well as for the staff and volunteers who provide direct services and care to them.

Author Acknowledgements

Cary Bach Donahou

With much gratitude, I'd like to give thanks to Mary for bringing us together and holding space for our voices, with courage and compassion. I'd also like to express my gratitude for the women I came to know through our vulnerability. You have all been a light in my life these past two years, may we always be that for one another. Most importantly to my daughters, without whom I'd never have had the courage to walk this path.

Susan Hamin

I want to express my gratitude to Mary for creating and offering this writers group and to the women I have been writing with for the past two years. They have allowed me to know their pain which allows me to see their strength and in turn mine.

Thanks to those who have offered me safety, compassion, and understanding. It is through those relationships I have recovered myself. Thank you to my daughter, always.

Keena Hildebrand

For my parents, who broke many generational curses and stood with me in my fire. For my children who have always been a source of light and love — often giving me the energy to continue fighting. For my husband who has supported my rage and passion at every step — never shying from the challenge. For all of the women in this book who have seen the tides of my rage swell through my eyes and witnessed me in a way that made me feel truly seen. Each of you inspires me. For Mary, who did all the hard parts and acts as a megaphone, amplifying our voices and giving us a place for healing. For RAINN, who has helped me to advocate and heal. Who has lifted the voices of survivors and provided the resources that save their lives. For Laura, with whom I have a bond with that many could not understand. I hope you found peace.

And, as I am learning, for myself.

ANGELA LORE

For my supportive husband, who continues to inspire me every day. You are really that person I can't live without. For my two sons and daughter-in-law, who let me know they are always there for me. For my parents who pray for me constantly– I am forever by your side. For my grandsons who are my constant source of joy, wonder, and laughter. For all the amazing women in our group, you've exposed me to some of the most thought-provoking and heartfelt writing, and for that I will always be grateful. And for Mary, you have been a constant source of blessings, love, and light for all of us. You are both my mentor and cherished friend. Lastly, for my black cat, Sunday—thank you for rescuing me.

MECKS MAC

Many thanks to RAINN for its support of survivors and for providing us the opportunity to participate in these writing workshops, without which this anthology would not exist. Thank you, Mary, for your leadership and your time.

GINGER T. REX

Thank God for GrahamBo, who adores and cherishes me, and for my brave and brilliant kids who are champions of courage. Thank you, Charlie, Jim, and Lesa for walking me through the fire. I count you as blessings. To my siblings who speak my language, I love you. Mary, I am grateful for your light and strength. Like moonlight on a dark night, you lit our way despite the costs and challenges you faced. To each member of our group, thank you for your kindness. We agreed that alone is not better, so we linked our arms to find healing through writing together. Finally, thanks to Amherst Writers & Artists Press for your valuable ink and to RAINN for giving us the space and place to do the work.

MARY SIMMERLING

I want to thank the brave women whose stories are in this book. I am deeply grateful to and for you. I admire and am humbled by your courage in coming forward to join me on this healing journey. I honor your divinity and would walk through fire with you any time. It is you who have made "Write Where We Belong" the force for healing that it is. I want to thank Scott Berkowitz, the founder and President of RAINN, who trusted me enough to join me in exploring the power of story with the members of the RAINN Speakers Bureau.

Also many thanks to my core team at Amherst Writers & Artists (AWA) – Sue Reynolds, Meadow Jones, Carla Hanson, Jan Haag, Susan Wingert, Gail Cunningham, Elizabeth Perlman, and the many incredible leaders at AWA who not only have supported and encouraged me on the journey to this anthology, but who came forward to honor the women's voices and stories and make this anthology the very best it could be. While I initially came to AWA to learn how to lead writing workshops grounded in social justice, what I found was a home filled with incredibly gifted and generous collaborators and mentors.

I am very grateful to Dr. Holly Silva, who has been an incredible source of support and healing for me and provided critical guidance on aspects of this anthology.

To my dear friend Jason Mark Yates, thank you for seeing us and reflecting back to us with your incredible gift of the song *Sunshine Through the Rain* in celebration of this anthology.

None of this would have been possible for me without the unwavering support, love, and editorial prowess of my husband Thomas. And of course, my greatest teacher, Kalven. Finally, to my late mother Marjorie — thank you for everything.

BIBLIOGRAPHY

Baikie, K. A., & Wilhelm, K. (2005). Emotional and physical health benefits of expressive writing. *Advances in Psychiatric Treatment,* 11(5), 338-346

Bluvshtein, M. (2017). *The Story — Alfred Adler and His Indivisible Psychology... His and Ours.* [Video file] Retrieved from Marina Bluvshtein | AdlerPedia

Cavell, Stanley. (1976). *Must We Mean What We Say?: A Book of Essays.* Cambridge. Cambridge University Press.

Chandler, G. E., Roberts, S. J., & Chiodo, L. (2015). Resilience intervention for young adults with adverse childhood experiences. *Journal of the American Psychiatric Nurses Association,* 21(6), 406-416. https://doi.org/10.1177/1078390315620609

Conti, P. (2021). *Trauma: The invisible epidemic: How trauma works and how we can heal from it.* Sounds True.

Costa A, Foucart A, Hayakawa S, Aparici M, Apesteguia J, et al. (2014). Your morals depend on language. *PLOS ONE* 9(4): e94842. https://doi.org/10.1371/journal.pone.0094842

Glass, O., Dreusicke, M., Evans, J., Bechard, E., & Wolever, R. Q. (2019). Expressive writing to improve resilience to trauma: A clinical feasibility trial. *Complementary Therapies in Clinical Practice,* 34, 240-246. https://doi.org/https://doi.org/10.1016/j.ctcp.2018.12.005

Hefferon, K. & Boniwell, I. (2011). *Positive Psychology: Theory, Research And Applications.* McGraw-Hill Education. http://ebookcentral.proquest.com/lib/adler/detail.action?docID=729517

Huberman, A. (Host). (2023, November 20). *A Science-Supported Journaling Protocol to Improve Mental & Physical Health* [Video]. YouTube

Keysar, B. & Costa, A. (2014, June 20). Our moral tongue. *The New York Times.* https://www.nytimes.com/2014/06/22/opinion/sunday/moral-judgments-depend-on-what-language-we-are-speaking.html

Lepore, S. J., & Smyth, J. M. (Eds.). (2002). *The writing cure: How expressive writing promotes health and emotional well-being* [doi:10.1037/10451-000]. American Psychological Association. https://doi.org/10.1037/10451-000.

Moor, A. (2010). She Dresses to Attract, He Perceives Seduction: A Gender Gap in Attribution of Intent to Women's Revealing Style of Dress and its Relation to Blaming the Victims of Sexual Violence. *Journal of International Women's Studies,* 11(4), 115-127. http://vc.bridgew.edu/jiws/vol11/iss4/8

Pennebaker, J. W. (1997). Writing About Emotional Experiences as a Therapeutic Process. *Psychological Science,* 8(3), 162-166. https://doi.org/10.1111/j.1467-9280.1997.tb00403.x

Pennebaker, J. W. (2012). *Opening Up: The Healing Power of Expressing Emotions.* Guilford Press.

Pennebaker, J. W., Kiecolt-Glaser, J. K., & Glaser, R. (1988). Disclosure of traumas and immune function: Health implications for psychotherapy. *Journal of Consulting and Clinical Psychology,* 56(2), 239–245. https://doi.org/10.1037/0022-006X.56.2.239

Pulverman, C. S., Boyd, R. L., Stanton, A. M., & Meston, C. M. (2017). Changes in the sexual self-schema of women with a history of childhood sexual abuse following expressive writing treatment. *Psychological Trauma: Theory, Research, Practice, and Policy,* 9(2), 181-188.

Rogers, P., Lowe, M., & Reddington, K. (2016). Investigating the Victim Pseudomaturity Effect: How a Victim's Chronological Age and Dress Style Influences Attributions in a Depicted Case of Child Sexual Assault. *Journal of Child Sexual Abuse,* 25(1), 1-19. DOI: 10.1080/10538712.2016.1111964

Sagi, B. (2021). "Only when it's written here": personal writing as testimony in the aftermath of childhood sexual abuse. *Journal of Poetry Therapy,* 34(3), 150-163. https://doi.org/10.1080/088 93675.2021.1921475

Schneider, P. (2003). *Writing Alone and With Others.* Oxford University Press.

Sexual Assault Prevention & Education Center. (2023). *What Were You Wearing (WWYW)* Installation. University of Kansas.

Sharma-Patel, K., Brown, E. J., & Chaplin, W. F. (2012). Emotional and Cognitive Processing in Sexual Assault Survivors' Narratives. *Journal of Aggression, Maltreatment & Trauma,* 21(2), 149-170. https://doi.org/10.1080/10926771.2012.639053

Siegel-Acevedo, D. (2021). Writing Can Help Us Heal from Trauma. *Harvard Business Review.*

Simpson, L. B. (2021). "Head of the Lake" [Song]. *Theory of Ice.* You've Changed Records.

Smyth, J., & Helm, R. (2003). Focused expressive writing as self-help for stress and trauma. *Journal of Clinical Psychology,* 59(2), 227-235. https://doi.org/10.1002/jclp.10144

Smyth, J., & Nobel, J. (n.d.). Creative, artistic, and expressuve therapies for PTSD. *Arts & Healing,* 1-7. chrome-extension:// efaidnbmnnnibpcajpcglclefindmkaj/https://www.artandheal-ing.org/wp-content/uploads/2015/07/PTSD-White_Paper_Smyth_Nobel1.pdf

Stuckey, H. L., & Nobel, J. (2010). The connection between art, healing, and public health: a review of current literature. *Am J Public Health,* 100(2), 254-263. https://doi.org/10.2105/ajph.2008.156497

Vagianos, A. (2017, September 15). Art exhibit powerfully answers the question 'What Were You Wearing?' *HuffPost.* https://www.huffpost.com/entry/powerful-art-exhibit-powerfully-answers-the-question-what-were-you-wearing_n_59baddd2e4b-02da0e1405d2a

van der Kolk, B. (2014) *The Body Keeps the Score.* Penguin.

Zelin, A. I., Walker, R. V., & Johnson, D. M. (2019). Cornered at a Bar: How Victim Clothing, Alcohol Intake, and Relationship With Bystander Impact Intention to Help. *Violence Against Women,* 25(10), 1163–1190. https://doi.org/10.1177/1077801218809948